QUIET POWER

THE GET-BACK IS GRACE

How I Led, Mothered, and Healed
Through the Loudest Divorce in Town

A Faith-Based Inspirational Memoir

Camela Guyton

ISBN: 979-8-234-05124-0

DEDICATION

To God,

Who revealed the truth with mercy and grace, Who held me tenderly when I felt alone.

Who broke me gracefully so I could be made whole again,

And who continually carries me through every storm with unwavering love.

Thank you for strengthening my faith when doubt tried to take hold,

For whispering peace into my restless heart,

For being my refuge and my rock when I felt weak and uncertain.

I place my full trust in You.

Knowing that your plans are perfect,

Your timing is perfect,

And Your grace is sufficient for every moment.

Through every tear, every prayer, every quiet surrender,

You lifted me higher, teaching me to walk by faith, not by sight.

You transformed my pain into purpose and peace,

My brokenness into beauty, And my fear into hope.

To my children,

You are my greatest blessings and my heart's deepest joy, You inspired me to keep going when I felt like giving up, You reminded me daily of the strength that comes from love, And you are the reason why I fought so hard to heal.

ACKNOWLEDGMENT

I would like to express my heartfelt gratitude to everyone who supported me throughout the journey of bringing this book to life.

A special thank you to Apostle Gretchel Dixon, whose guidance and expertise were instrumental in helping me navigate the publishing process. Your support made this dream a reality.

I am also deeply grateful to Minister Aisha Williams for the incredible creativity and care put into designing the book cover. Your work captured the spirit of this book perfectly.

Thank you both for your invaluable contributions.

INTRODUCTION

I didn't break loudly.

I didn't fall apart in front of everyone.

Instead, I led. I mothered. I stayed quiet when I wanted to scream, And through it all, God walked with me through the fire.

Like Shadrach, Meshach, and Abednego, I went through a furnace of pain, divorce, betrayal, and emotional wreckage, but I didn't come out ruined. Not a hair on my head was singed. The fire didn't leave its mark on me because God was there, carrying me through every moment.

This book is not just my story of heartbreak and healing; it is the testimony of how God turned my greatest test into a powerful witness. What was meant to harm me, God used for good, building strength, grace, and purpose not only for me but for every woman who reads these pages. The real "get-back" isn't about revenge.

It's about grace. It's about choosing faith when everything around you seems to be falling apart. This is how I made it!

Welcome to my journey….quiet, powerful, and full of God's unshakable love.

TABLE OF CONTENTS

PART I

THE UNRAVELING

GRACE IN THE REVEAL

It was 2020 when I went to God in prayer with a heavy heart. I remember saying, "Lord, please reveal whatever it is You want me to see and know. Whatever it is, I'm ready. I can feel in my spirit that something is off. I need You. I trust You to show me the truth, and I believe with all my heart that You will take care of my children and me.

God didn't just reveal the truth. He shattered the illusion I had been clinging to for far too long. In His mercy, He uncovered what had been hidden in darkness, not to destroy me, but to set me free.

What followed was a whirlwind of emotions I wasn't prepared for: fear, heartbreak, confusion, betrayal, frustration, and deep, aching embarrassment. It felt like the ground had been ripped out from underneath me. And to make things even more complicated, the world was in crisis as well. With everything shut down and life happening behind closed doors, there was no escaping the weight of what I was feeling. I didn't know which way was up or how I would make it through, but I knew I wasn't alone.

I knew then that something had to change. I needed space to breathe, to process, to hear from God without the noise of chaos around me. That season was not easy. It was filled with quiet battles, private tears, and difficult choices. But it was in that space, in that stillness, that I began to reclaim my voice, rediscover my worth.

This season marked the breaking of something I thought I couldn't live without, but it also marked the beginning of something far greater: a journey toward healing, wholeness, and peace. It was the first step on a path I never expected to walk, but one that would ultimately lead me closer to God and to the woman He created me to be.

For so long, my identity had been wrapped up in being a wife, a mother, and a school leader. As an Assistant Principal at the time, I was used to taking care of everyone else, solving problems, managing crises, and being the dependable one. At home and at work, I was constantly pouring out. And while I never truly forgot who I was, I often placed my own joy, my passions, and the things that made *me* feel alive on the back burner. I told myself I'd get to it later.

But in that sacred space with God, I realized that later had finally come. I began to reconnect with the woman who laughed, who dreamed, who had desires outside of duty. Not just the one who held everything together, but the one who was allowed to just be.

And in that moment, I knew without a doubt that I would need God like never before. Not just in quiet moments of prayer, but every single day, every hour, every breath. This was a season that would require constant surrender, relentless faith, and an unshakeable reliance on Him. I was broken, deeply and completely, and only His grace could hold me together for the journey ahead.

A Letter to My Mom, Sister, Sister in Love, and Special Cousin

Thank you for being my safe place during a season that shook me to my core. When life unraveled, and I could barely hold myself together, you stood in the gap. You were my strength when I didn't have any left. You listened, even when there were no words. You prayed for me and with me, reminded me of who I was, and never let me forget who God is.

You covered me in love that didn't demand details. You offered comfort without judgment. In your own quiet way, each of you helped me breathe when I felt like I was drowning. Whether it was a phone call, a text, a visit, or just the silence of knowing someone who gets it. You helped hold me up while God held my heart.

You didn't try to fix me. You loved me, and that love gave me space to heal. In my most broken place, you reminded me that I didn't have to be strong all the time. That it was okay to fall apart… as long as I fell into the arms of the One who could put me back together.

Your presence was a gift. Your support was sacred. I will never forget the way you showed up for me every single time. You were part of the grace God sent to help carry me through.

Thank you for being my tribe. Thank you for being God's hands and heart in my life.

With all my love,

Camela (Cammy)

Songs That Carried Me During This Season

1. **"**Gracefully Broken**"** by Tasha Cobbs Leonard
2. **"**Yesterday**"** by Mary Mary
3. "Help Me" by Vanessa Bell

Prayer

Lord,

Thank You for seeing me even when I felt invisible. Thank You for holding me together when everything around me was falling apart. In the moments when I've put everyone else first and silenced my own voice, You reminded me that I matter too. Teach me how to care for myself without guilt, how to rediscover joy without apology, and how to walk in the identity You gave me, not just as a role, but as Your daughter. Help me to make space for stillness, for healing, and for the version of me that's been patiently waiting to breathe again.

Amen

Affirmation

Even in the unraveling, I am not undone. Truth may shake me, but it will not break me. I release what no longer serves me, and I make room for peace. I am worthy of healing, worthy of joy, and worthy of a life built on truth. I am more than what I've lost. I am who I am becoming.

Scripture

"The Lord will fight for you; you need only to be still." ***Exodus 14:14 (NIV)***

Journal Prompt

- In what ways have you put yourself, your joy, or your needs on the back burner?

- What are some simple ways you can begin reconnecting with the woman God created me to be beyond your roles and responsibilities?

THE STRENGTH IT TOOK TO STAY SILENT

God knew exactly what I needed during the storm. Even when I didn't know how I would make it through. In His grace, He shielded me from the public eye at a time when I was at my most vulnerable state. Because it was during COVID, everything slowed down. The world shut down, and in that stillness, God gave me space to begin healing without the pressure to explain myself, show up polished, or wear the mask I was so used to.

I was blessed to work remotely for several months. To be exact, it was six months of quiet, privacy, and grace. It was during that time that I learned how to care for myself in a new way. After my administration duties and "homeschooling my children," I would take long walks every day. Sometimes I would walk alone, with just gospel music in my ears, other times, with my sisters or close friends. They walked with me, prayed with me, and encouraged me when I felt like I couldn't keep going. I was in constant prayer, clinging to the word. I read daily devotionals, studied scripture, listened to virtual sermons, and immersed myself in truth. God became my lifeline.

Even though I was crumbling on the inside, I couldn't afford to fall apart on the outside. I had children who needed stability. I had to lead with strength at work. I had to be steady, even when I didn't feel it. So I took care of myself, not for luxury, but for survival. I didn't have the luxury to break in front of my kids. I had to protect their peace, their innocence. They never knew what I was going through, and that was intentional. I carried it quietly so they wouldn't have to.

I returned to work in the Fall. What my colleagues didn't know was that I was carrying the weight of grief, heartbreak, and silence. But I didn't say anything. I was the strong one. The fixer. The leader. The one who always kept it together. And no one expected me to be falling apart. I went through the entire school year without letting them know I was going through a divorce.

But even in that silence, God was strengthening me. He was teaching me that silence doesn't mean weakness; it can be sacred. It can be strategic. It can be survival. And sometimes, the strongest thing a woman can do is say nothing... and let God do everything.

A Letter to My Children

There are things I haven't told you. Things I've carried quietly to protect your hearts and your peace. I want you to know that every day, I prayed for you, even when I was hurting inside. I kept my tears hidden so you wouldn't have to worry. I worked hard to be strong, so I could shield you from the storms around us.

You are the greatest blessing in my life. Even when things felt uncertain, God never stopped guiding me. He used that strength to hold us all together. I hope you see, one day, that sometimes being strong means being silent and trusting God to do the work we can't see.

I want you to remember that it's okay to feel your feelings, to ask for help, and to lean on God every single day. Your joy, your peace, and your happiness will always be my greatest prayer.

Know this: I love you fiercely, unconditionally, and forever. And no matter what, God's grace is carrying us, and will carry you, through every season of life.

With all my love,

Mom

Songs That Carried Me During This Season

1. "Still Able" by James Fortune and FIYA
2. **"**Better Days**"** by Le'Andria Johnson
3. "I Trust You" by James Fortune and FIYA
4. "You're Bigger" by Jekalyn Carr

Prayer

Lord,

Thank You for shielding me when I couldn't shield myself. Thank You for quieting the world so I could begin to hear You clearly. In the moments when I had to stay strong for everyone else, You were the strength holding me up. You surrounded me with peace, with people, and with Your presence. Even when I couldn't say what I was going through, You heard the cries of my heart. Help me to continue protecting what matters without silencing my own needs. Teach me that it's okay to care for myself while caring for others. And remind me, Lord, that even in silence, You are speaking. Even in stillness, You are moving.

Amen

Affirmation

My silence is not weakness; it is wisdom. In the stillness, I find strength. I protect what matters most while allowing grace to protect me. Even when no one knows my battle, God fights for me in private. I am strong, I am seen, I am sustained. My quiet is powerful. My peace is sacred. And my healing is mine.

Scripture

"God is our refuge and strength, an ever-present help in trouble." **Psalm 46:1 (NIV)**

Journal Prompt

- What are the areas in your life where you've stayed silent to protect others?

- How did God show up for you in that silence?

- In what ways can you give yourself permission to prioritize your own healing while still showing up for those you love?

LEADING A SCHOOL, ENDING A MARRIAGE

There's a unique kind of exhaustion that comes from pretending you're okay while leading others through a storm, especially when your own life is unraveling behind the scenes.

The year I became a principal was supposed to be a celebration, a career milestone, a fulfillment of purpose, a chance to finally lead in the way I had prepared for. But instead of stepping into it with confidence and joy, I walked in carrying a heart that was breaking and a life that felt like it was falling apart behind closed doors.

What made this season even more difficult was that everything that could go wrong in a school year did. I started the year in quarantine, sick with COVID, alongside my two daughters, who were also quarantined with me. I was leading a school from my son's bedroom, trying to manage a team virtually, make major decisions, and set the tone for a new year, all while caring for my sick children and battling through the illness myself. I felt completely isolated, overwhelmed, and stretched to my physical and emotional limits. I was someone's principal, someone's boss, someone's co-worker, but I was also someone's mama. I couldn't fall apart! Not when little eyes were watching. Not when tiny hands still needed to be held. So I poured myself out in every direction, nurturing my children through sickness, leading my school through crisis, and managing my own emotional unraveling behind closed doors. I did it all with a smile. Not because I was okay, but because I had to be.

I had to build a leadership team from the ground up, learn the school's culture, create systems, and provide answers for things I was still trying to figure out myself. I was managing high expectations, balancing unseen pressure at home, and stepping into meetings with a smile while silently praying I wouldn't fall apart. No one knew what I was carrying, and I couldn't afford for them to know.

Every morning, I showed up early before the sun came up and before my children awoke from their sleep. Not because I had to, but because I needed to. That quiet time became sacred. I'd sit in my office, close the door, open my devotional, and pour my heart out in prayer. Worship music filled the room, and *"You Know My Name"* by Tasha Cobbs played on repeat like it was my personal anthem.

That song reminded me that even though I felt invisible, forgotten, or broken, God still saw me. He knew my name. He knew my pain. He knew the weight I was silently carrying.

There were days I led on autopilot, smiling in meetings, encouraging teachers, supporting families, and solving problems—while silently praying, *"Lord, please hold me together."* Being busy helped me cope. It distracted me from the pain. But the truth was, work had become a way to avoid fully facing what I didn't want to admit.

I often stayed at school later than I needed to. Not for the job, but for the escape. The school building became a refuge from the reality I was afraid to sit with. I buried myself in responsibilities….answering emails, helping others, planning events, until there was nothing left of me but exhaustion. And yet, I kept showing up.

I showed up for students who needed hope. I showed up for teachers who needed leadership.

I showed up for a school that needed direction. And I showed up for my children, ensuring their lives stayed as stable as possible, even while mine felt anything but.

I was getting maybe four hours of sleep most nights, spending my days solving problems and my nights wrestling with emotions, unanswered questions, and silent prayers.

There were moments when I felt like I was drowning in responsibilities. The school year was relentless. Every single day seemed to come with a new fire to put out, a crisis to manage, a phone call that changed the course of the day, a challenge that tested every ounce of patience, wisdom, and strength I had left. I barely had time to process one thing before something else would go wrong. It was as if I was constantly bracing for impact. And yet, even in the middle of that chaos, God kept showing up.

One morning, after an especially difficult week, I reached out to my pastor and his wife, who, by divine design, lived right across the street from the school. Without hesitation, they came into my office and stood with me. They prayed over me, the school, my leadership, and my mind.

In the days leading up to that moment, I had started to question everything. I wondered if I had made a mistake by accepting the role of principal during such a turbulent season. I questioned if I was truly called to lead at all. The pressure felt unbearable, and the weight of both my personal and professional battles made me feel like I was drowning.

But in that moment of prayer, God gently reminded me that He wouldn't put more on me than I could bear. That I was not here by accident. That he trusted me fully to lead a school, even in the middle of a storm. He had equipped me. He had called me. And even though I doubted my worth, He never doubted me.

Through every "fire" I had to put out, through every decision I didn't feel equipped to make, through every moment I wanted to give up, God was present, placing people, peace, and power in my path. Quiet reminders that I was never truly alone.

I didn't have the luxury of shutting down. I didn't have the option of breaking down. Somehow, in all of it, God never let me fall. He gave me just enough strength to get up each morning. He gave me wisdom when I had none. He gave me peace in moments I thought I'd break.

And most of all, He reminded me that I wasn't alone even when I couldn't speak the full truth of what I was enduring. This was the hardest year of my professional life and the hardest year of my personal one, too. But looking back, I realize something profound: God sustained me in the silence. He strengthened me in the shadows, and He gave me the ability to lead, not in my own strength, but through His. Prayer works, and I got through this school year only because of His grace.

A Letter to My Pastor and First Lady

Thank you from the depths of my heart for being God's instruments in my life during one of my darkest seasons. Your unwavering support, prayers, and presence brought me comfort when I felt overwhelmed and alone.

You stood with me not just as spiritual leaders but as friends—reminding me of God's promises, lifting my weary spirit, and helping me find strength to keep going. Your prayers were a shield around my family and me, and your faithfulness inspired me to trust God even when I doubted myself.

I am grateful for the countless mornings you prayed with me, the scriptures you shared, and the love you showed without hesitation. You have been a beacon of God's grace and peace, and I thank God every day for you both.

With love and gratitude,

Cammy

Songs That Carried Me During This Season

1. "Made a Way" by Travis Greene
2. "Same Grace" by William Murphy
3. "Thank You (Lord for All You've Done)" by Walter Hawkins
4. "Thank You for It All" by Marvin Sapp
5. **"Good News"** by Vanessa Armstrong

Prayer

Lord,

You are my strength when I am weak, my peace when the storms rage, and my anchor when life feels like it's falling apart. Thank You for carrying me through seasons where I didn't think I could carry myself. Thank You for trusting me to lead, even when I felt unqualified and undone. When I doubted myself, You reminded me of who I am. Keep guiding me, keep sustaining me, and help me never forget that you are near, even in the chaos.

Amen

Affirmation

Even when the world sees strength, God sees my struggle, and he sustains me. I lead through pain, but I am never alone. I am not held together by performance, but by purpose. In every unseen battle, he fights for me. In every silent tear, he is near. I am proof that grace works in motion….leading, loving, and living, even when breaking. Even in pain, God's purpose presses on, and His power carries me through.

Scripture

But he said to me, 'My grace is sufficient for you, for my power is made perfect in weakness.' Therefore, I will boast all the more gladly about my weaknesses, so that Christ's power may rest on me." **2 Corinthians 12:9 (NIV)**

Journal Prompt

Think back to a season where you had to keep showing up while silently falling apart.

- What did you need during that time?

____
____
____
____
____
____

- How did God show up for you, even when no one else knew what you were going through?

____
____
____
____
____
____

- What would you say to that version of yourself now?

____
____
____
____
____
____

PART II

PROTECTING MY CHILDREN

TELLING THE KIDS (OR NOT)

There's a sacred kind of silence that only a mother understands, the kind where you carry the weight of truth quietly, not because you're hiding, but because you're protecting.

But from the very beginning, my priority was clear: our children.

As a mother, I always wanted to raise my children differently from how I was raised. I committed early on that no matter what happened, I would not argue in front of my children. I would not involve them in "grown folks' business." I would never force my children to carry the weight of adult issues.

We showed up at school events, shared meals, and moved through the motions of co-parenting as we began this new adventure. While it may have looked functional from the outside, it was a daily emotional and spiritual battle for me. I was still leading a school, parenting three children, going to church, reading my Bible, attending counseling, and holding onto God for dear life, all while quietly processing the loss of a marriage that had already ended in my heart.

There were moments I wanted to scream, cry, or give up. But I couldn't. My children deserved a sense of normalcy. They deserved peace in their home, even if mine felt like anything but peaceful.

Eventually, my children began to notice things. The questions started slowly.

Their words stopped me in my tracks.

Not because they were disrespectful, but because they revealed something I hadn't fully acknowledged: they *knew* more than I realized. They were watching. They were wondering. And they were quietly piecing things together in their own way.

That broke my heart! Not because I had failed, but because I thought I was shielding them when, in reality, they were absorbing the unspoken truth. I had spent so much energy trying to keep everything "normal" that I underestimated how perceptive and emotionally aware children can be.

And that's when I realized protection isn't the same as pretending. Shielding them doesn't mean silencing everything. It means choosing the right time, the right way, and the right words and trusting God to fill in the rest.

So I waited. I didn't wait out of fear. I waited out of love. I waited because I knew I couldn't lead them through something I hadn't fully processed myself. My faith, at the time, wasn't yet strong enough to carry all of us at once. I was barely breathing emotionally, spiritually, and mentally.

So I chose myself first. Not in selfishness but in wisdom. Just like the flight attendants say on every airplane: "Put your oxygen mask on first, before assisting others." I needed to breathe again. I needed to heal, to process, to cry, to get therapy, to talk to God, and to rebuild myself from the inside out. I needed God to strengthen me so that when the time came to have that conversation, I could offer my children truth and peace. I could offer honesty and security.

Because here's what I know now: You don't always have to reveal everything to protect your children. But you do have to parent with wisdom, patience, and prayer. And when the time is right, God will give you the words, the strength, and the peace to lead them through it with love.

Song That Carried Me During This Season

1. "All I Need" by Brian Courtney Wilson

Prayer

Lord,

Thank You for trusting me with the gift of motherhood, even in seasons where I feel unsure or undone. Thank You for giving me the wisdom to know when to speak and the grace to remain silent when needed. Help me lead my children with truth and love—not fear. Help me trust that You are also parenting them through this journey, just as You are parenting me. When I feel overwhelmed or uncertain, remind me that You are my guide, my peace, and my ever-present help.

Amen

Affirmation

Choosing to heal is not selfish; it's sacred. I do not rush what requires grace. I wait with wisdom, not fear. God is strengthening me so I can strengthen them. I protect my children not with silence, but with discernment. I am not failing; I am faithfully preparing.

Scripture

All your children will be taught by the Lord, and great will be their peace."
Isaiah 54:13 (NIV)

Journal Prompt

- In what ways have you tried to protect your children by staying silent?

- What have they noticed or asked that made you realize they're more aware than I thought?

- What would it look like to trust God to help you lead your child(ren) through this season… with truth, grace, and wisdom?

KEEPING THEIR WORLD INTACT WHILE MINE FELL APART

There's a kind of strength that doesn't come with applause or recognition. It comes in quiet moments, when you choose not to answer questions that would shatter your children's peace, when you carry the weight of rumors and whispers without passing them on, when your heart is breaking, but your love for them holds everything together.

This was the delicate balance I lived in. While the world around us swirled with speculation, noise, and misunderstanding, my deepest desire was to preserve something sacred for my children: their sense of stability, security, and emotional safety. I knew I couldn't shield them from everything, but I was determined not to let chaos shape their childhood.

There were days when they asked questions I wasn't prepared to answer, hard questions, uncomfortable questions, painful questions. Sometimes the questions came from things they heard at school, from adult conversations they had overheard, and questions from their friends. At other times, I wasn't even sure where the questions came from. They caught me off guard, pierced me deeper than I could show. But even in those moments, I knew my role wasn't to respond out of emotion or hurt....it was to cover them.

So I chose to answer with wisdom, not wounds. I gave them what peace I could, often pointing them back to prayer, back to God, or encouraging conversations with their father when the answers belonged to him. I didn't speak poorly. I didn't explain the details. I simply protected the space between what they asked and what they weren't ready to carry.

Behind the scenes, I was constantly in prayer. When things felt too heavy or when the process dragged on longer than I could bear, I created space to talk to God privately. And though I didn't always have the words, God always heard the cries I couldn't say out loud.

I know my children noticed more than they said. I know they worried when they saw my bedroom door closed. I know they wondered when I needed space or left the house for a few hours just to gather myself. I saw it in their eyes, even when they didn't say a word. I also know that my silence, my restraint, and my choice to rise each day wasn't just about survival. It was about planting seeds of faith and strength in them, too.

This chapter is not about the people who stirred confusion or the voices that tried to invade our peace. It's about the God who silenced every storm within me so I could create calm for my children. It's about the grace that gave me restraint when I could have spoken out of pain. It's about the strength to choose what is best for them. Even when it cost me the comfort of release.

My world may have been falling apart, but theirs didn't have to. And if nothing else, I pray they remember this: that even when life was loud, their mother fought quietly, loved fiercely, and trusted God to hold what she could not.

A Letter to My Children

There are some things in life that are too heavy for young hearts to carry, and as your mother, I did my best to carry them for you.

You may not have known everything I was going through, and that was intentional. It wasn't because I didn't trust you or because I didn't want to be honest. It was because I love you more than words could ever express, and I wanted to protect the light in your hearts while mine was learning how to shine again.

I know you noticed things I didn't explain. I know you had questions I didn't always answer. And I know there were moments that made you wonder more than you said. But please know this: every choice I made was from a place of love and intention. I wasn't hiding the truth; I was holding space for your peace.

In the moments when my door was closed, or I needed quiet, it wasn't because I was shutting you out. It was because I was going to God for strength, so I could keep showing up for you with love, with patience, and with grace.

You are the reason I kept going. You are the reason I stayed grounded when life felt unsteady. Your laughter, your love, your presence... those were the bright spots in some of my darkest days.

One day, if and when you face your own storms, I pray you remember what I hope I showed you: that strength is quiet sometimes, that peace is worth protecting, and that God is faithful......even when life doesn't look the way we hoped it would.

I love you with my whole heart. And I always will.

With all my love,

Mom

Prayer

Lord,

Thank You for the strength to protect my children even when I felt unprotected. Thank You for guiding my words when silence was the wisest answer, and for holding my heart when it ached in private. Help me continue to lead my children with gentleness, wisdom, and grace. Teach them to turn to You in their own questions, just as I turned to You in mine. May our home always be a refuge, one filled with peace, safety, and the steady reassurance of Your love.

Amen

Affirmation

Even when the noise around me is loud, I choose peace. Even when I'm uncertain, I walk in wisdom. I am a safe place for my children and a stronghold of grace. I don't have to explain everything to protect what matters. God is my refuge, and He is covering every part of my family's story.

Scripture

"She is clothed with strength and dignity; she can laugh at the days to come."
Proverbs 31:25 (NIV)

Journal Prompt

- What emotions have you had to quietly carry in order to protect others?

____

____

____

____

____

____

- What did you learn about your own strength while doing so?

____

____

____

____

____

____

- How can you continue creating a peaceful environment for your child(ren), even when you're still healing yourself?

____

____

____

____

____

____

HELPING MY KIDS HEAL WITHOUT FORCING FORGIVENESS

There comes a point in every mother's life when you realize your strength isn't just for you, it's for them. For your children. For the legacy of peace, you want them to carry, even when life hasn't been peaceful.

The day I finally sat down to tell my children the truth about our divorce is a day I will never forget. It wasn't a moment I rushed into. It was one I prayed for, prepared for, and worked toward healing. My counselor had given me a clear assignment: it was time. Time to stop pretending, time to let go of the illusion of stability, and time to start helping my children walk in truth.

I wasn't just responsible for the truth; I was responsible for how it was delivered, when it was delivered, and whether it was delivered from a healed heart or a hurting one.

So, after much prayer, I called my children into the room and shared what I had feared for so long: we were divorced. Their reactions were different, but equally heavy. There were tears. There was silence. There was visible pain.

But I was ready. Not because I had all the answers, but because I had done the work to stand in peace. I prioritized my healing first. I had spent months in prayer, in counseling, and in quiet surrender to God so that when the time came to support them, I wouldn't be leading from brokenness. I would be leading with wisdom.

I had a plan in place. I had already enrolled my children in therapy. I knew my daughter would be expressive and bold in her emotions, and I knew my son might retreat inward to protect his emotions. Both reactions were valid. Both required grace. And both would need a safe space to unravel and rebuild.

We brought in prayer. My pastor stayed connected with us by coming to the house to pray and covered us. We started doing Bible study as a family, not because we had it all together, but because we didn't. Because the word was the only thing strong enough to hold us when life felt shattered.

A Letter to My Children

There is no pain like watching your children hurt and feeling like there's nothing you can do to take it away. But I want you to know everything I did, I did with you in mind. I waited to tell you the truth because I wanted to be strong enough to carry you through it. I chose healing so that I could be whole for you when the time came to walk through hard truths together.

I never stopped praying for you. I never stopped covering you. And I never stopped believing that God would take this pain and turn it into purpose.

You may never fully understand all the choices I made. But I hope you remember that I loved you through all of it with grace, with protection, and with relentless hope. I wanted you to grow up knowing that you don't have to become bitter to be strong. That you don't have to return hurt with hurt. That forgiveness is not weakness, it's freedom.

One day, when you face your own trials—and you will—I pray you remember how we got through ours: with prayer, with love, and with God.

With all my love,

Mom

Songs That Carried Me During This Season

1. "I Believe" by Shawn McLemore
2. "The Battle is the Lord's" by Yolanda Adams
3. "He's Able" by Voices of Unity *featuring* Darwin Hobbs

Prayer

Lord,

Thank You for being my defender. When I wanted to retaliate, You reminded me that revenge belongs to You. You saw every moment I stayed kind when I could've been cold. You heard every cry I didn't speak aloud. Thank You for honoring the posture of my heart and surrounding me with peace that doesn't make sense. Help me continue to choose grace over retaliation, wisdom over emotion, and faith over fear. Remind me that forgiveness is not for them, it's for *me*! And as I walk forward, may I never forget: You are my justice, my joy, and my "get-back."

Amen

Affirmation

I don't need revenge to feel victorious.

God's grace is my get-back.

I am not defined by how others treat me. I'm defined by how I rise in truth, walk in love, and trust in God's provision.

While they wonder how I'm still standing, I'll keep giving God the glory because he is my source, my strength, and my shield.

Scripture

Do not take revenge, my dear friends, but leave room for God's wrath, for it is written: 'It is mine to avenge; I will repay,' says the Lord." **Romans 12:19 (NIV)**

Journal Prompt

- Who do you need to release in order to fully receive the peace and purpose God has for you?

- What blessings has God already given you that proves He can handle what you no longer need to hold?

- What does grace look like for you in this season and how can you show it without compromising your healing?

PART III

THE QUIET WORK OF HEALING

WHEN GRACE MEETS MY MESS

There were moments when I didn't respond the way I wanted to, or the way I would have coached someone else to. My faith was real, but so was my pain. In the privacy of our home, during some of the most tense and heartbreaking moments, I lost my temper. I said things I wasn't proud of.

I acted out of deep hurt, not out of healing.

For a fleeting second, it felt like release, but it wasn't. The ache was still there. And afterward, I felt the weight of not just what had been said, but what had been witnessed. My children saw more than I ever wanted them to see. I was trying to hold everything together, but I wasn't always graceful. Sometimes I was just surviving. And survival looked messy.

I also began to realize how exhausting it is to fight with the flesh. Every outburst, every moment of impatience, was really me choosing flesh over faith. And that battle wore me out. I thought I was strong enough to handle it all, but God kept reminding me, "*Be still. Let Me work.*"

The truth is, I didn't always listen. There were times I tried to get in God's way, to fix things myself, to push my own will instead of waiting for His. And each time, I was reminded, sometimes gently, sometimes through painful lessons, to sit down somewhere and let Him be God.

What I didn't know in those moments was that He was working on me. Every setback, every time I got "knocked down" by him, was really God teaching me how to stop fighting battles that weren't mine to fight. It was shaping me, preparing me, humbling me because this wasn't just about my healing. This was about the testimony He was building in me so I could one day help another woman who felt the same exhaustion, the same war between flesh and faith.

Over time, I learned the power of patience. I learned the strength that comes from listening to God's voice instead of my own emotions. And most importantly, I learned that grace doesn't just clean up our mess, it walks with us through it, again and again.

Grace didn't mean perfection. It meant starting over. It meant being human in front of my kids, apologizing when I needed to, and still pointing them back to the God who was helping me grow. My flesh got loud. My emotions took over. But grace… grace had the final say!

A Letter to God

There were moments when my flesh was louder than my faith. I lashed out in ways I wasn't proud of. I acted from hurt rather than healing, from anger rather than patience. I tried to control things I shouldn't have. I rushed, I pushed, I forgot that You were already at work.

Forgive me for the times I didn't wait on You. Forgive me for the times I let pride or pain rule my words and my actions. Thank You for being patient with me, for not leaving me in the mess, and for showing me that grace doesn't demand perfection—it simply asks me to return to You.

Lord, teach me to listen when You whisper, to wait when You are working, and to trust that Your timing is perfect—even when my heart wants it done yesterday. Help me to surrender my battles, my pride, and my fears into Your hands. Let my testimony be proof that You can turn the chaos of flesh into the calm of faith, and the exhaustion of trying to control everything into the joy of trusting You.

Thank You, God, for always having the final say. Thank You for showing me that grace is bigger than my mistakes, stronger than my emotions, and deeper than my pain. I give You all of me—flesh, faith, failures, and all.

With love,

Cammy

Songs That Carried Me During This Season

1. "Great is Your Mercy" by Donny McClurkin
2. "Something Happens (Jesus)" by Bishop Paul Morton Sr.
3. "Still Able" by James Fortune and FIYA
4. "I Need Your Glory" by James Fortune and FIYA Prayer

Prayer

Lord,

Thank You for teaching me that I don't have to control everything. Forgive me for the times I tried to do Your work for You. Help me to wait with patience, to listen to Your voice, and to surrender my battles into Your hands. Give me the wisdom to choose faith over flesh, and peace over striving.

Amen

Affirmation

I don't have to fight battles in my flesh. God fights for me. His grace is stronger than my weakness.

Scripture

"The Lord will fight for you; you need only to be still." **Exodus 14:14 (NIV)**

Journal Prompt

- Where in your life are you still trying to "fix it yourself"?

- Write down one area you can surrender to God this week and ask Him to help you trade your flesh for faith.

THERAPY, JOURNALS, AND CONVERSATIONS THAT HELPED ME FIND PEACE

Some seasons of life demand more than prayer alone; they demand guidance, accountability, and the willingness to face hard truths. For me, that season came during one of the most challenging times of my life. I was blessed with three lifelines: two pastors who served as father figures and a professional counselor. These three became my walking Bibles. When I didn't have the strength to open the Word myself, they spoke it into my life, reminded me of God's promises, and gave me the guidance I desperately needed.

These conversations were not always easy. Sometimes they told me things I already knew, but hearing them aloud stung. Yet, I am eternally grateful because those hard truths helped me grow and carry lessons into my future. One thing that set each session apart was that I always walked away with *work to do for myself.* They gave explicit, actionable steps to help me heal, grow, and realign my life with God's purpose.

It was during this season that I began journaling and learned to fast spiritually and prune what no longer belonged in my life. I remembered a conversation from 2018, before the divorce, when I asked one of my pastors how to discern what is Divine versus what is Demonic. He wrote me a response that I would return to during this season, and it became a guidepost for navigating spiritual, emotional, and practical decisions:

Divine is God! Demonic is the Devil! God will always do what is necessary to grow us, bringing peace within and around us. The enemy will try to disturb and destroy. When it's God, He reassures you, and the path becomes clear. When it's demonic, confusion and distraction follow. Pray, journal, and ask God to help in the pruning process—removing what does not belong, while guiding you into what He intends for your life."

Journaling became my medicine. I wrote at work before my day started, and at home before bed. I reflected on lessons from my counselors, on what I learned from devotions by local authors, and on my personal journey. These pages became a mirror of growth, spiritual, emotional, personal, and professional. Years later, returning to these journals and seeing how far God had brought me left me in awe. Truly, He is a miracle worker. The growth, the transformation, the healing—I am so grateful.

Through therapy, journaling, fasting, pruning, and godly conversations, I discovered a profound truth: intentional reflection and accountability are essential tools for healing. God uses people, prayers, and the act of writing to restore, guide, and prepare us for the next season of life.

The Apostle Paul serves as a biblical example of this practice. While imprisoned, Paul wrote letters that later became the New Testament, preserving wisdom, encouragement, and guidance for generations. Like Paul, I learned that writing down reflections, prayers, and lessons allows God to work through your experiences, providing clarity, growth, and a testimony for others. These journals became my lifeline and eventually planted the seed for the book I knew God was calling me to write for women going through divorce.

Looking back, I see how God orchestrated everything—the counseling, the hard conversations, the journaling, the fasting, the pruning. The lessons I learned and the work I did for myself built a foundation for my spiritual, emotional, and personal growth. Reading through these journals years later reminds me of God's faithfulness and the miracle of transformation.

Letter to My Counselors

Thank you! Thank you for walking with me through one of the most challenging seasons of my life. Your words, guidance, and accountability were lifelines when I could not find my own strength. The "homework" you gave me, the journaling, the reflections, the actions, became tools that transformed my life.

You reminded me that healing is intentional, that growth requires effort, and that God works through those he places in our paths. I am so grateful for your wisdom, your patience, and your unwavering belief in my ability to grow. Because of you, I have healed, I have learned, and I continue to walk in HIS purpose.

With deepest gratitude,

Cammy

Songs That Carried Me During This Season

1. "Take Away" by Yolanda Adams
2. "God Provides" by Tamela Mann
3. "Something God" by William Murphy
4. "Still Able" by James Fortune and FIYA
5. "Standing in The Need" by John P. Kee

Prayer

Heavenly Father,

Thank You for sending people into my life who spoke Your Word when I could not speak it myself. Thank You for the gift of journaling, reflection, and meditation, which allows me to see Your faithfulness over time. Lord, help me continue to grow in wisdom, strength, and faith as I reflect on my journey. Thank You for showing me that healing comes through intentional actions, godly counsel, and Your Word. May I continue to use the lessons, journals, and guidance You've given me to live fully and purposefully. In Jesus' name.

Amen

Affirmation

I am committed to my growth and healing. Each reflection, each journal entry, each godly conversation brings me closer to the woman God created me to be. I honor my journey and embrace the blessings that come from intentional reflection and accountability.

Scripture

"Write the vision; make it plain on tablets, so he may run who reads it." **Habakkuk 2:2 (ESV)**

"I have fought the good fight, I have finished the race, I have kept the faith."

2 Timothy 4:7 (ESV) (Paul reflecting the power of journaling and preserving faith)

Journal Prompt

- Write a letter to your future self, five years from now.

- What do you hope she thanks you for?

GOD SENT THE GIRLS

These women were not just my friends; they were my lifeline. In a season when everything in my world felt heavy, they were light. They offered me the rare gift of presence without pressure, allowing me to simply be without explanation.

When I was with my girls, it wasn't always about venting or unpacking the weight of what I was going through. Sometimes, I just needed to sit in a space where I didn't have to lead, mother, or explain. And they gave me that. Whether we were at brunch, on a last-minute girls' trip, or just sitting around a living room, they gave me space to exhale.

There were moments we laughed until we cried, not because everything was okay, but because we were okay in that moment. We cracked jokes, reminisced about old memories, and yes, eventually, we even laughed at some of the stories I once cried over. Not out of bitterness, but because healing had made room for humor. And when you're on the other side of something that almost broke you, laughter is a sacred kind of grace.

My friends didn't always know it, but God was using them. They reminded me that I was still human, still whole, and still worthy, even in the middle of grief. Their presence became part of His provision. They didn't try to fix me; they just stayed close. Some days we talked deeply, other days we didn't talk at all. But the consistency of their love created a safety net I didn't know I needed.

There were times I did open up, when I needed to process what I was carrying or laugh at the irony of it all. And they listened with love, never judgment. They often told me how much they admired my strength, how they couldn't believe how well I was co-parenting, and how I still showed so much grace in situations that would've broken them. What they didn't always realize is that I was opening up not just for me, but for them, too! I wanted them to see that it's possible to go through something devastating and still come out whole. That faith really does sustain you. And that healing, while personal, doesn't have to be private.

I never wanted my vulnerability to just be a moment; I hoped it would be a mirror. That maybe, if one of them ever faced heartbreak, betrayal, or transition, they would remember my story and feel less alone. That they would know faith isn't reserved for the perfect, it's for the broken, the tired, the trying, and the ones who are still finding their way.

My girls gave me joy when joy felt far away. They made me feel normal when everything in my world felt upside down. And even now, when we gather, there's still laughter, still love, and always grace.

Because of them, I could return home to mother, to lead, to serve, refreshed and reminded that I wasn't alone. They carried me in the quiet when my strength ran out. They cheered for me in the dark when the spotlight was gone. They loved me back to life!

A Letter to My Girls

Thank you!

For the laughs that made my stomach hurt.

For the wine nights, the brunches, the girl trips, and those last-minute "get dressed, we're going out" texts that saved me more times than you'll ever know.

In a season where my world was quietly crumbling, you became a soft place to land. You gave me space to exhale. You never forced me to talk, but when I did, you listened without judgment. You reminded me that I was still me, even when I didn't recognize myself. You pulled me out of the shadows of shame and helped me step into the light again.

Thank you for taking me away when I needed to escape. Thank you for pouring into me when I felt empty. Thank you for being fun, honest, protective, and present. Those moments… dancing, laughing, roadtripping, or just sitting in silence, were more than distractions. They were healing. They were sacred.

You didn't let me stay broken. You reminded me I was still worthy. You didn't ask me to pretend. You let me be soft, silly, silent, and still be seen. What you gave me was sisterhood in its purest form.

Thank you for standing with me in the fire and helping me come out without the smell of smoke.

I love you forever!

Cammy aka Camela aka Cam

Songs That Carried Me During This Season

1. "Grateful" by Hezekiah Walker
2. "Still Say Thank You" by Smokie Norful
3. "Lord You Are Good" by Todd Galberth
4. "Fill Me Up Overflow (live)" by Tasha Cobbs

Prayer

Lord,

Thank You for the women You placed in my life who held me up when I couldn't stand on my own. Thank You for sacred sisterhood—for joy in the middle of sorrow, for light in the darkest hours, and for laughter that reminded me I was still alive. Bless them the way they blessed me. Fill their cups as they have poured into mine. Remind me that rest is holy, that fun is necessary, and that I don't have to carry the weight of healing alone.

Thank You for the grace that shows up through people.

Amen

Affirmation

God sends what I need in every season, even in the form of friendship. I am allowed to rest, to laugh, and to feel joy, even in hard times. Replenishment is not a luxury. It's part of my survival. My healing matters, and I do not have to heal alone.

Scripture

"Two are better than one, because they have a good return for their labor: If either of them falls down, one can help the other up." **Ecclesiastes 4:9–10 (NIV)**

Journal Prompt

- Who did God use to carry you in your hardest season?

- How did moments of joy or rest help you hold onto yourself?

- In what ways can you continue making space for replenishment in your life?

PUBLIC SHAME, PRIVATE STRENGTH

There were seasons when it felt like my life had become the town's favorite conversation. Whispers traveled faster than truth, and assumptions seemed louder than my actual voice. I made a choice. I chose not to feed the fire.

Instead of scrolling, reading, or responding, I stepped away from the noise. I learned quickly that I could not heal if I kept my ear tuned to whispers. The voices of others could not guide me; only the voice of God could.

Still, let me be honest: turning your ear away from rumors and idle talk is one of the hardest things the flesh will ever have to do. Our natural desire is to listen, defend ourselves, or even clap back. But discipline requires silence. Discipline requires restraint, and discipline requires faith that God sees what we cannot.

When I stopped listening to the chatter, I started hearing God more clearly. What could have distracted me, I turned into devotion time. The energy that could have been wasted on rumors, I poured into prayer, fasting, journaling, and filling my spirit with his promises.

Yes, I was being talked about. But I also knew that being talked about was different from being torn down. In fact, every word spoken against me became a reminder of the One who sustains me. The same God who shut the lions' mouths for Daniel was shutting out the noise so I could hear Him more clearly.

And here's the truth: whispers do not define us. God does. Public shame will never outweigh private strength when that strength is rooted in Him.

That season was not meant to destroy me; it was meant to discipline my focus. And with each test, my testimony grew stronger!

A Letter to Myself

I know how heavy it feels to walk into a room and sense that people have already spoken your name. I know the sting of whispers, the distraction of rumors, and the temptation to defend yourself. But I want you to know this: you don't have to prove your worth to anyone. God has already called you His.

Let the chatter pass. Let the whispers fade. Lift your head and keep walking. Your story is not in their mouths; it is in God's hands. Every word spoken against you is an opportunity to show the quiet power of grace. Keep your eyes fixed on Him, and He will carry you through with dignity.

With love and strength,

Camela

Songs That Carried Me During This Season

1. "God Favored Me" by Hezekiah Walker
2. "Fill Me Up" by Tasha Cobbs
3. "You Will Win" by Tasha Cobbs
4. "You Brought the Sunshine" by the Clark Sisters

Scripture

"The Lord will fight for you; you need only to be still." **Exodus 14:14 (NIV)**

Journal Prompt

- When have you felt the sting of being misunderstood, judged, or talked about?

____

____

____

____

____

____

- How did you respond in that moment, and how would you like to respond if it happens again?

____

____

____

____

____

____

- What disciplines (prayer, fasting, scripture, affirmations) can you lean on when you're tempted to listen to rumors or defend myself?

____

____

____

____

____

____

LETTING GO WITHOUT NEEDING TO BE RIGHT

Sometimes in life, we think closure is required for healing. We wait for an apology that never comes, a conversation that never happens, or the "perfect ending" that ties up every loose end. But ladies, the truth is, closure does not always arrive neatly packaged from someone else. Closure is a choice you make within yourself. It's you deciding to close the chapter so that God can begin writing the next one.

If we stay stuck waiting for validation from others, bitterness and negativity begin to take root. That weight will not only hold you down, but it will also poison your ability to trust and move forward. The real battle isn't with another person; it's with the parts of us that want to control the outcome.

One of the most powerful tools you can use in this season is silence. Being silent does not mean you are weak. It means you are wise. Every time you choose silence instead of arguing, you are protecting your peace. You are setting boundaries. You are refusing to invest energy in conversations that don't matter or in people who don't have the power to define your worth.

Think about it: the time you spend going back and forth, replaying scenarios in your head, or waiting on closure could instead be invested in yourself, your self-care, your healing, and most importantly, your relationship with God. Every ounce of energy you waste trying to be "right" is energy you could be using to grow into the woman God designed you to be. Remember, it's not about them, girl...... It's about *you*!

When you surrender the fight to God, something shifts. Suddenly, it's no longer about winning arguments, proving your point, or forcing justice. It becomes about peace. It becomes about trusting that God sees what was done, He knows the truth, and He has the final say. His Word reminds us, "The Lord will fight for you; you need only to be still" (Exodus 14:14).

That is the true victory… not the last word, but lasting peace. Not getting even, but getting aligned with God. When you let go, you make space for Him to usher you into your *winning season*! And this winning season is not about someone else losing, it's about you becoming. It's about you stepping into the fullness of who God has called you to be.

Remember the promise in Romans 8:37: "In all these things we are more than conquerors through Him who loved us." You don't have to fight for closure. You don't have to force people to see your side. You simply need to release, surrender, and trust that God's justice and God's peace are greater than anything you could manufacture on your own.

This is the victory: not control, not being right, but walking boldly into the future God has prepared for you. It's time to win, God's way!

Letter to Myself

I am so proud of you! You have shifted from needing to be right to choosing peace. You've learned that letting go is not losing. It's winning in the most powerful way. Every time you chose silence instead of fighting back, you protected your spirit. Every time you surrendered instead of forcing closure, you opened the door for God to move in your life.

You no longer waste energy trying to prove yourself to anyone. That energy now belongs to you, for your healing, your growth, your joy, and your walk with God. You've realized that it has never been about them… it has always been about *you*!

This journey is about your happiness, your peace, and your freedom. You've already won because you are becoming the woman God created you to be. Stand tall, smile big, and know this truth deep in your soul: You are walking in your winning season.

Love always,

Me

Songs That Carried Me During This Season

1. "Change Me" by Tameka Mann
2. "Made a Way" by Travis Greene
3. "Lord Do It for Me" by Zacardi Cortez
4. "It's Working" by William Murphy

Prayer

Heavenly Father,

Thank You for reminding me that I don't need to fight to be right. I don't need to chase closure or force justice. You are my defender, and You fight battles I cannot see. Lord, teach me the power of silence when words won't bring peace. Help me guard my spirit, set healthy boundaries, and protect my energy. Remind me daily that my worth is not tied to arguments, outcomes, or anyone else's approval. Strengthen me to choose peace over pride, surrender over control, and Your will over my own. I release every situation that has drained me, and I step boldly into the season You've prepared for me. This is my winning season. In Jesus' name.

Amen

Affirmation

I release the need for closure and the desire to always be right. My peace is more valuable than any argument. I choose silence, surrender, and trust in God's plan. I am free, I am whole, and I am already winning.

Scripture

"The Lord gives strength to his people; the Lord blesses his people with peace."
Psalm 29:11 (NIV)

Journal Prompts

- Where in your life are you still waiting for closure from someone else, and how can you begin to create closure within yourself?

____

____

____

____

- In what situations do you need to practice silence to protect your peace?

____

____

____

____

- How can you redirect the energy you spend on arguments or "being right" into self-care and deepening your relationship with God?

____

____

____

____

- What does your "winning season" look like, and how can you celebrate the ways you are already winning?

____

____

____

____

PART IV

THE LIFE I BUILT FROM THE ASHES

WHEN THE HOUSE IS QUIET, AND YOU'RE FINALLY ALONE

There comes a moment in life when the noise finally stops, and the world you've been navigating, the arguments, the chaos, the constant tension, fades into silence. That quiet can feel strange at first, almost unfamiliar. But slowly, you begin to realize the gift it brings freedom.

In the stillness, you can breathe. You can reflect. You can honor your growth and acknowledge how far you've come. There's no need to compete, explain, or justify. You can simply exist, and in that existence, you discover joy, peace, and pride in yourself.

Solitude allows you to reconnect with who you truly are. It's a space to care for your body, mind, and spirit without interruption. It's a time to rest, to pray, to listen, and to simply be. Even when loneliness visits, it is softened by the knowledge that you no longer carry the weight of chaos or expectation that doesn't belong to you.

This quiet teaches gratitude. It teaches patience. It teaches that peace is not only possible—it is yours for the taking when you release control, step away from unnecessary conflict, and allow God to guide your steps.

In those moments, you remember that lightness, the lightness of walking in freedom, of giving yourself permission to rest, of choosing joy over tension. It's in the quiet that you truly hear your own heart, your own spirit, and the gentle voice of God guiding you forward.

Letter to God

Thank You for the quiet. Thank You for the moments when I can finally breathe, reflect, and simply exist without distraction or chaos. Thank You for guiding me to a place where I no longer carry the burdens that were never mine to bear.

Help me to continue to embrace this stillness as a gift—a time to rest, to heal, and to grow. Teach me to use this solitude to reconnect with You, to honor my own heart, and to walk in the lightness and freedom You provide. I am grateful for every peaceful moment and for the clarity and joy that come from being fully present in Your presence.

With gratitude,

Cammy

Songs That Carried Me During This Season

1. "It's Not Over" by Israel and New Breed
2. "Peace" by Juanita Bynam
3. **"Forever"** by Jason Nelson

Prayer

Lord,

Thank You for the gift of quiet and solitude. Help me to use these moments to rest, reflect, and grow closer to You. Teach me to treasure the peace that comes from walking in freedom and trusting You. May my heart always be grateful, my spirit light, and my life aligned with Your will.

Amen

Affirmation

I embrace the gift of quiet. I am free, I am peaceful, and I am whole.

Solitude restores me and strengthens my spirit.

Scripture

"Be still, and know that I am God." **Psalm 46:10 (NIV)**

Journal Prompt

- What does quiet and solitude feel like for you? How can you embrace moments of stillness to reflect, rest, and reconnect with yourself and God?

RECLAIMING MY IDENTITY, NOT JUST MY LIFE

For so long, my identity was wrapped up in the titles I carried... wife, mother, principal. Those roles gave me purpose, but they also consumed me. When life, as I knew it fell apart, I realized I had to rediscover who I was without the labels, without the noise, without the constant demand to show up for everyone else.

So, I began to pray. My prayer was simple but powerful: "Lord, give me a healthy work-life balance. Teach me how to care for myself the way I care for others." God answered—not overnight, but through small, intentional steps.

I started dating someone new... me. For the very first time, I took myself to the movies. I sat at a restaurant table, ordered my own meal, and enjoyed my own company. I booked hotel rooms for one, just to rest in peace and quiet. I went on road trips where the only agenda was to breathe. Sometimes I would escape to a friend's house just to get away from the noise of life. Those moments weren't about loneliness; they were about reclaiming my space.

I said "yes" to things I used to decline. I went to women's conferences and retreats where I could sit in rooms filled with encouragement, empowerment, and truth. I spoiled myself, not with things, but with experiences. I tried new foods, listened to different kinds of music, and gave myself permission to discover what made me happy and what made me uneasy. It was all part of learning *Cammy* again.

Through these choices, I realized something profound: reclaiming my identity wasn't about filling the void left by others. It was about learning to stand whole in my own presence, knowing that I was enough.

A Letter to Every Woman Healing

I see you! I see the woman who has spent so much of her life pouring herself into everyone else, mother, wife, leader… always showing up, always giving, always carrying the weight of others. I see the woman who sometimes forgets she deserves the same love, care, and attention she gives so freely.

I want you to know this: it is not selfish to get to know yourself again. It is not wrong to choose your peace, your joy, and your growth. Reclaiming your identity is not about leaving anyone behind or shutting the world out. It's about stepping fully into the woman God created you to be… whole, vibrant, and free.

Take the time to explore what makes you smile, what makes your heart feel light, and what restores your soul. Pray. Reflect. Rest. Treat yourself with the same kindness and generosity you give to others. And when someone asks for your time or attention, give it from a place of abundance, not depletion.

This is your season! Your time to heal, to laugh, to dream, and to rediscover the beauty of simply being you. You are worthy of joy, of rest, of experiences that feed your spirit. And you do not need a title, a relationship, or anyone's approval to validate that worth. God and you are enough!

So, sister, I encourage you: step into your space boldly, without guilt, without hesitation, and with a heart open to discovery. Let this be the chapter where you fall in love with yourself again, because when you do, everything else aligns with grace.

With love and encouragement,

Cammy

Songs That Carried Me During This Season

1. "You're Bigger" by Jekalyn Carr
2. "New" by Tye Tribbett
3. "Big" (Extended Version) by Pastor Mike Jr.

Prayer

Heavenly Father,

Thank You for reminding me that my worth is found in You alone. Help me continue to prioritize my peace, my health, and my joy without guilt or hesitation. Show me new ways to love myself as You love me, and help me walk boldly in my identity, rooted in Your grace.

Amen

Affirmation

I am worthy of joy, rest, and discovery. I do not need a title or another person to define me. God and I are enough!

Scripture

"Instead of your shame, you will receive a double portion, and instead of disgrace, you will rejoice in your inheritance. And so you will inherit a double portion in your land, and everlasting joy will be yours." **Isaiah 61:7 (NIV)**

Journal Prompt

- Think about the roles and titles you carry.

- Who are you beyond them?

- Write about one thing you want to do just for yourself this week, something that makes you smile, brings you peace, or reminds you of who you truly are.

SETTING BOUNDARIES WITHOUT SETTING FIRE

One of the hardest parts of co-parenting, or navigating any broken relationship, is learning how to set boundaries without letting your emotions dictate your decisions. When parents argue in front of children, or use them as pawns in their disputes, the damage is real and long-lasting. I've seen it firsthand, and research confirms it: children thrive when parents are kind, respectful, and cooperative, even if they don't like each other.

As an educator, I know the stakes. Boundaries are not about being vengeful, petty, or cruel; they are about protecting your peace, your values, and, most importantly, your children.

Here's the truth: boundaries are about facts, not feelings. If you make decisions from anger, hurt, or frustration, you will burn yourself every single time. I learned this the hard way. To protect your heart and your home, you must be willing to put your feelings aside and focus on what's right, not what's convenient or emotionally satisfying in the moment. In other words, keep the main thing on the main thing, the children.

Setting boundaries means:

- **Aligning your choices with your values, beliefs, and morals.** If a decision doesn't match who you are at your core, it's okay to say no.
- **Processing before responding.** Don't rush to answer when emotions are high. Take time to pray, reflect, and gain clarity.

- **Prioritizing what's best for the children.** Decisions are not about "winning" or getting back at someone; they are about creating stability, safety, and love.
- **Knowing when to step back.** Sometimes the wisest choice is to remove yourself from the drama, allow space for God to work, and respond with intention, not reaction.

I cannot stress this enough: boundaries are protection, not punishment. They are a shield for your peace, a map for your values, and a compass for your family's future. When you set them with clarity and kindness, you model integrity, respect, and emotional intelligence, not just for your children, but for yourself.

Remember, boundaries are guidelines rooted in truth. Over time, as relationships evolve and situations change, you can adjust, but never compromise your values, your morals, or your children's well-being.

Setting boundaries aren't easy. It takes courage. It takes patience and practice. It takes faith. But when done right, it keeps your heart from burning, your children from being caught in the crossfire, and your life aligned with the God-given principles you hold dear.

Letter to God

Thank You for guiding me through the process of setting boundaries. Thank You for teaching me that I can stay firm without being vengeful, clear without being cruel, and protective without being controlling. Lord, I know that my emotions can sometimes try to dictate my decisions, and I am grateful that You remind me to pause, reflect, and seek Your will.

Please continue to help me make choices that align with Your way and Your timing, not my feelings or frustrations. Help me to respond with wisdom, patience, and grace in every situation, especially when it comes to co-parenting, relationships, and protecting my children.

Thank You for helping me set boundaries that honor my values, morals, and the purpose You have for my life. Lord, let these boundaries not only safeguard my peace, but also model integrity, respect, and faithfulness for my children. May every decision I make reflect Your love and guidance, and may my life continue to point others to Your wisdom.

I trust You, Lord, to lead me, strengthen me, and direct my steps. Keep my heart aligned with Your purpose, and help me walk boldly in the freedom and peace that comes from trusting You completely.

With love and gratitude,

Cammy

Songs That Carried Me During This Season

1. "You Reign" by William Murphy
2. "Yes" Reprise by Shekinah Glory
3. "He's Working It Out for You" by Shirley Cesar
4. "Enough" by Anthony Brown and Group Therapy

Prayer

Lord,

Give me the wisdom to set boundaries that honor You. Help me respond with patience, clarity, and kindness, even when it's hard. Protect my heart and my children from conflict and guide my decisions so that they reflect my faith, integrity, and love.

Amen

Affirmation

I set boundaries with clarity and love. I protect my peace and my children without compromising my values.

Scripture

"Let your 'Yes' be 'Yes,' and your 'No,' 'No.'" **Matthew 5:37 (NKJV)**

Journal Prompt

- Where in your life do you need to set clear boundaries, especially for the sake of your child(ren)?

- How can you respond with facts, faith, and values rather than emotion?

FORGIVING WITHOUT FORGETTING

Forgiveness is one of the hardest lessons life will ever demand of us. Especially when the betrayal comes from someone you once built a life with, shared memories with, and thought it would be forever. Forgiveness doesn't come easy. It feels unnatural at first, but it is necessary if you want to walk in peace, healing, and wholeness.

For me, this was one of the hardest seasons of my life. Yet it became one of the most freeing. I learned that forgiveness was never about excusing what happened or pretending it didn't hurt. Forgiveness was about keeping my heart soft. I didn't want to become bitter or allow pain to spill over into my children, my relationships, or my future.

Forgiveness was like shedding old skin, peeling away layers of anger, resentment, and disappointment, and stepping into a new covering of strength and grace. It was not about giving someone else a "win." It was about choosing myself, my peace, and my future.

My mother played a vital role in this process. She reminded me, again and again, that forgiveness was non-negotiable if I wanted to live free. She shared her own experiences and lessons, and she held me accountable when I didn't want to hear it. I'm so grateful for her persistence, because she helped me see that unforgiveness only blocks blessings, but forgiveness opens the floodgates of God's favor.

Jesus makes it plain in **Matthew 6:14–15**:

"For if you forgive other people when they sin against you, your heavenly Father will also forgive you. But if you do not forgive others their sins, your Father will not forgive your sins."

Forgiveness is not optional; it's a command, and it's tied to our own freedom.

I prayed for the strength to forgive, over and over. And as hard as it was, I even began to pray for the one who hurt me. Praying for someone who wounded you deeply feels impossible, but it is one of the most powerful acts of release.

Forgiveness is not forgetting. Forgiveness is saying: This will not control me anymore. I'm moving forward. I'm letting God handle the justice, while I step into peace.

I also discovered something incredible: when you forgive, God can turn your enemy into your footsteps. Every trial, every betrayal, every person who tried to derail me became part of the path God was building for my growth, my testimony, and my future ministry.

Letter to My Mother

Thank you! Thank you for introducing me to God! Thank you for holding me accountable when I wanted to hold on to anger. Your wisdom, your reminders, and even your tough love helped me walk into freedom.

You showed me that forgiveness wasn't about the other person; it was about me, my peace, and my future. You taught me that holding on only blocks what God is trying to release in my life. Because of you, I chose forgiveness, and it set me free.

I honor you for being my soundboard, my guide, and my example. I carry your lessons with me always, and I am so grateful that God gave me a mother who not only told me the truth but lived it.

With all my love,

Your Daughter

Songs That Carried Me During This Season

1. "Proof" by Pastor Mike Jr.
2. "Your Love" by Wiliam Murphy
3. "You Are Great" by Juanita Bynum
4. "He Always Makes a Way" by James Fortune & FIYA

Prayer

Father,

Thank You for forgiving me again and again, even when I fall short. Lord, help me to extend that same grace to others. Remove bitterness from my heart and replace it with peace. Teach me to forgive, not because they deserve it, but because You command it and because I need it for my own freedom. Give me the courage to pray for those who hurt me and the wisdom to trust You with the outcome. I release the pain, and I step into the blessings that forgiveness unlocks. In Jesus' name.

Amen

Affirmation

I release bitterness and resentment. I forgive, not for them, but for my freedom, my peace, and my future.

Scripture

"Be kind and compassionate to one another, forgiving each other, just as in Christ God forgave you." **Ephesians 4:32 (NIV)**

Journal Prompts

- Who in your life do you still need to forgive, and what is holding you back?

- How has unforgiveness affected your peace, joy, or relationships?

- What blessings or breakthroughs might be waiting on the other side of your forgiveness?

- How can you hold yourself accountable (or who can hold you accountable) to live out forgiveness daily?

WHAT I WOULD TELL A WOMAN GOING THROUGH THIS NOW

You've made it to the final chapter. But more importantly, you've made it this far in your journey of healing, growth, and faith. Let me remind you, you are not alone. God is with you every step, and there is a village of women, friends, and loved ones ready to walk this path with you.

I want you to know something critical: healing is for you, not for anyone else. It's okay to prioritize yourself. It's okay to take space. It's okay to say no. You are worthy of peace, joy, and restoration, and your journey matters.

I also hope this chapter brings awareness to those who may have caused pain, intentionally or unintentionally. My story is shared not to shame, but to illuminate the journey of healing. Sometimes people hurt others because they are hurting themselves. My prayer is that through these pages, someone who has caused pain might gain understanding, surrender to God, and seek the help they need to heal. After all, we know hurt people hurt people—but that, my friends, is another story for another book.

There will be days when you aren't okay. There will be moments of doubt, fear, or heaviness. That's normal. You may have to put on a "face" for work, events with your children, or other obligations. That's okay. In those moments, turn to prayer, scripture, and affirmations. Let God carry your worries, remind you of His glory, and strengthen your faith.

I give God all the glory for my healing, for the confidence He has placed in me, and for the words and wisdom He has given me to empower others walking through similar struggles. It is by His grace that I can guide, encourage, and inspire—to show that even in the darkest seasons, there is light, hope, and restoration.

- **Stay grounded in your values and beliefs:** never allow anyone to change your character.
- **Limit or remove social media:** silence the noise and avoid triggers.
- **Cancel the noise:** gossip, negativity, or anyone feeding "bad thoughts" into your mind.
- **Protect yourself on bad days:** silence yourself from people and silence your phone if needed.
- **Surround yourself with a healing village:** supportive friends, prayer partners, women's ministry, or a group that listens without judgment.
- **Take girls' trips** even when you don't feel like it.
- **Laugh a lot!** Joy is medicine for the soul.
- **Find a hobby** that brings peace, creativity, or fun into your life.
- **Do something for yourself every day**—even if it's just 15 minutes before going into the house. Be yourself, not just a mom or employee.
- **Read scriptures and affirmations** in moments of weakness; let God's Word ground you and remind you of His grace and faithfulness.
- **Journal consistently** and revisit past entries to see how far you've grown and healed.
- **Surround yourself with positive thoughts and people**—if they aren't positive, it's okay to let them know and even let them go.
- **Enroll in therapy . . . HEAL!**

Dear Sister,

Healing is for you, and you deserve every moment of it. Protect your peace. Embrace joy. Laugh. Pray. Surround yourself with people who lift you up, and let God guide every step. Let this be your season to rediscover yourself, to reclaim your power, and to walk boldly in faith.

You are stronger than you think, and your story, your healing, can inspire others. Take it one day at a time. Trust the process. Trust God. And know that your journey is far from over; it is just beginning!

With love and faith,

Cammy

A Song to Start Your Healing Journey

1. "Heal" *(Extended Version)* by Jamal Roberts

Prayer

Lord,

Thank You for walking with me through this journey of healing. Help me trust You completely, even in the days I feel weak or weary. Surround me with Your peace, guide my steps, and protect my heart from negativity. Teach me to embrace joy, laugh freely, and prioritize my own healing. Let Your Word and Your presence be my foundation, today and every day.

Amen

Affirmation

I am healing. I am growing. I am not defined by my past, but by the strength and grace God gives me today.

Scripture

"Have faith in God. Truly I tell you, if you have faith as small as a mustard seed, you can say to this mountain, 'Move from here to there,' and it will move. Nothing will be impossible for you." **Matthew 17:20 (NIV)**

Journal Prompt

- What are three things you can do this week just for your peace and healing?

- Which scriptures or affirmations will you turn to when you feel weak or overwhelmed?

- How has God shown up in your journey so far, and what progress are you proud of today?

CLOSING

As you close this book, remember: your journey of healing, growth, and rediscovery is just beginning. You are not defined by the past, by others' choices, or by the pain you've endured. You are defined by your courage, your faith, and your willingness to rise, again and again, with grace. Keep praying, keep journaling, keep laughing, and keep honoring yourself. Your story is far from over!

I give God all the glory for my healing, for the confidence He has placed in me, and for the words and wisdom He has given me to empower other women walking through similar struggles. It is by His grace that I can guide, encourage, and inspire, to show that even in the darkest seasons, there is light, hope, and restoration.

And while this chapter may be ending, life has a way of opening new doors. Who knows what God has next? Perhaps there's another story waiting to be told, a season of love, joy, and connection that will challenge and delight you in new ways. For now, walk boldly, trust Him fully, and know that your healing has prepared you for every blessing yet to come.

STAY CONNECTED

With

Camela Guyton

www.iamcamela.org

Email: aaaconsultantgroup@gmail.com

www.ingramcontent.com/pod-product-compliance
Lightning Source LLC
LaVergne TN
LVHW020653100826
845148LV00012B/2473

* 9 7 9 8 2 3 4 0 5 1 2 4 0 *